Two Roads, Two Rooms

An introduction to the TrueFaced Experience

by Bill Thrall, Bruce McNicol and John Lynch

Two Roads, Two Rooms

An introduction to the TrueFaced Experience

by Bill Thrall, Bruce McNicol and John Lynch

Leadership Catalyst Inc./TrueFaced
8283 N. Hayden Road – Suite 275
Scottsdale, AZ 85258
Toll Free: 888-249-0700
www.TrueFaced.com

VISION
Every person experiencing the freedom of a TrueFaced™ life.

HISTORY
Established in 1995, Leadership Catalyst Inc./TrueFaced is recognized as an international resource for helping readers, leaders and groups discover the many freedoms of their identity, by learning to live TrueFaced™. It is our prayer that one day, tens of thousands of communities around the globe will experience the freedoms of living authentically as the norm in all their key relationships. God is using TrueFaced™ resources to nurture remarkable transformation in leaders, teams, marriages, churches and cultures.

ISBN: 978-1-934104-05-7

Editorial Team: Toben Heim, John Lynch
Creative Team: Rod Gipson, Amber Ong
Kakimoto, Alan McCuller

Printed in the United States of America

For more information on TrueFaced™ resources
call 888-249-0700 or visit us at www.TrueFaced.com

"Grace—an exquisite word carrying the power of God for new covenant transformation. But that power depends on seeing all the dimensions of grace. The vulnerability of the authors, life stories of grace people, and the careful attention to theological foundation make TrueFaced a book to treasure. As you read with your heart and your life, you'll enter into the joy of your salvation!"

—GERRY BRESHEARS, PH.D., professor of theology, Western Seminary, Portland, Oregon

"Integrity, the consistency between inner life and outward life, is the essential character trait of a leader. The authors, by stripping away the false outward masks that hide the inner life, are stressing an essential feature of integrity. May many enter into the Room of Grace they describe."

—DR. J. ROBERT CLINTON, professor of leadership, Fuller Theological Seminary

"Make this the very next book you read. Rarely does a new work address issues that speak so deeply to the heart. TrueFaced is an outstanding, truly life-changing book."

—LUIS PALAU, evangelist and broadcaster; author, *Stop Pretending* (Cook)

"Masking the truth about yourself benefits no one—most significantly, you. Come clean, confess honestly, hope unswervingly, and begin living a grace-faced life! This book will help you reach that trustworthy goal."

—DR. STEPHEN A. MACCHIA, founder and president, Leadership Transformations, Inc.; author, *Becoming a Healthy Church* and *Becoming a Healthy Church Workbook*

"TrueFaced is a compelling invitation to pursue authenticity. This is a wonderful, liberating book full of truths that will encourage all of us to be and reveal who we really are—the people God made us to be. What a powerfully relevant message for our time!"

—DR. CRAWFORD W. LORITTS JR., author, speaker, radio host; associate director, Campus Crusade for Christ, U.S.

"TrueFaced helped me to continue the important journey in learning to live based on who God says I am. As I read, I was forced to lay down the book and ask myself some hard questions. It took me to places of honesty that were uncomfortable, but I emerged cleansed, ready to rest in God's love and assurance."

—BILL HULL, author, *Jesus Christ Disciple Maker*, *The Disciple-Making Pastor*, and *The Disciple-Making Church*

"While actors are at their best when they are lost in the role and are not themselves, people are at their best when they confront the illusion of the role and are themselves. By exposing the futility of masks and the power in grace, TrueFaced is an invitation to understand the true meaning of 'being oneself.'"

—DR. ROD K. WILSON, president, Regent College, Vancouver, Canada

"This book is like a miraculous mirror—it shows us our self-imposed mask of hypocrisy and how to replace it with our true identity in Christ."

—HENRY W. HOLLOMAN, professor of systematic theology, Talbot School of Theology, Biola University; author, *The Forgotten Blessing*

"The principles taught in TrueFaced will help you, as they have me, in discovering the freedom of trusting God with who you are while providing authenticity in your relationships with God and others. I will use TrueFaced as a guide in helping people grow in trust and spiritual maturity as they embrace God's liberating grace."

—COMMISSIONER LAWRENCE R. MORETZ,
The Salvation Army, New York

"Leadership Catalyst portrays authenticity as the key to open our hearts to the transforming work of the Holy Spirit. Thrall, McNicol, and Lynch challenged me to embrace more fully the experience of love so I would be safe to strip away my masks of self protection. Taken seriously and prayerfully, you will not be left unchanged."

—DR. JUDY TENELSHOF, associate director,
The Spirituality Center, Hilltop Renewal Center

"This book is for Christians who seek to be authentic in their walk with Christ and with others. If you don't see yourself all too clearly in the engaging stories, then you might in response to the penetrating questions. By the time you finish, you will look more to love and grace than ever before."

—ROBERT C. ANDRINGA, PH.D., president,
Council for Christian Colleges & Universities

Introduction to Two Roads, Two Rooms

You've picked up a copy of the Two Roads, Two Rooms message. Without much risk of hyperbole we can tell you that you've stumbled onto a truly life changing document. It's just a short story really; an allegory, an extended metaphor. Whether it has been watched, listened to, or read on a page, it has rocked tens of thousands of us to our very core. It has brought hope and deep joy back to believers of all ages. It has been used to draw non-believers to this God they had always secretly believed might exist.

These pages describe nothing less than a revolution God is bringing to the Church. We are awakening to a restoration of how we are free to see ourselves in Christ. This is nothing less than a repudiation of the caricature of God we've been taught or taught ourselves. This distortion has kept us tied down, guilt-ridden, weary, lonely and isolated from each other. We've seen God as disgusted by our failures and have been left trying to somehow earn our way back into His favor. Most of us sadly came to believe that while we are justified through faith by grace, somehow we must mature and heal by some other means. We have become the "buck-up" people. And though it hasn't worked we didn't know another way. So, we've just learned to try harder.

But the day of self-righteous, religious performing for cheap applause truly is coming to an end. It has brought us nothing but enhanced skills in hiding, proving, striving, posturing and bluffing. Many of us, all over the world, have grown desperately tired of it. It is amongst such that God has been well pleased to begin this revolution to our radical historical faith of putting "no confidence in the flesh."

It is a shocking, incredible discovery that my best efforts have never been enough—to please God nor accomplish His will. This revelation allows me, maybe for the first time, to trust God with my maturity, healing and destiny in the same way I trusted Him for my salvation. It is a wild invitation to freedom. It is an invitation to discover a Power inside of me greater than I ever dreamed. It is an invitation to put my full trust in an intimately wonderful God as big as I once dared to believe He was.

In this story, we are confronted with a crossroads in our Christian journey—a single path that splits into a choice of two. A giant sign points in two directions: *Pleasing God* or *Trusting God*. They represent our initial heart motivation to live the rest of our lives. The *Pleasing God* path leads to *Striving Hard to be All God Wants Us to Be*, into the *Room of Good Intentions*. Here, I am *Working on My Sin to Achieve an Intimate Relationship with God*. It is an excruciatingly wearying walk. We try everything to make it work. In our moment of desperation God offers us the path of *Trusting God*, which leads us to *Living out of Who God Says I Am*, into the *Room of Grace*. In this room, I am *Standing with God, with My Sin in Front of Me, Working on it Together*. And I can finally take a full breath.

The thought that my sin is not between God and me, sounds heretical, too good to be true. It's the way we've always seen it, right? Yet, eventually the picture of Jesus with His arm around me captivates my soul. We are looking at my sin together, while He is saying, "I know kid. I've known before the world began. And I'm not angry. I'm crazy about you." This undoes me. And from that moment on I am unwilling to go back to any other manner of living.

One of the greatest gifts of this story is its ability to give a new language to describe what I've always thought, but didn't know how to communicate what I thought the Bible taught and couldn't seem to find anyone who saw it the same way.

It also gives me a visual, a picture of my journey. For I've been in both, the Room of Good Intentions and the Room of Grace, more than once. So, the story gives me a visual means of finding my way back home when I've stumbled back into the old dead teaching of good intentions. When shared, this picture gives us a way to help others back home too!

Finally, this story helps us find fellow journeyers who have been looking all their lives for such a Room of Grace. We hand this story to others we love. We can't stop talking to each other about this new/old way of living. At first we feel subversive, almost guilty, like we shouldn't dare be risking such claims. Then we find ourselves looking into our friend's eyes, saying, *"You too? You believe this?"* And then we can't stop talking to each other about it.

After this message settles in, there are usually at least these three inevitable responses:

First: *"Why have I wasted so much time in lies that have kept me in bondage?"*

Second: *"Why haven't I been told this before?"*

Third: *"How do I help free others to the Room of Grace?"*

Yep. Welcome to our world. This is all we do at Leadership Catalyst/TrueFaced. We invite tired and beaten up pilgrims into an Environment of Grace, the Room of Grace. And we try to help them nurture and sustain such an environment for those who have never tasted it.

This message is only a starting point. We've got dozens of resources to help a family, community, marriage or business live this way of life. But for now, enjoy the walk. Don't read it over and over. Put it down and go find someone else to read it, too. Some will not be affected. They will say something like, "Well, that was nice. But I don't get it. What's the big deal?" But others will sit stunned, reading words that agree with what Christ has been promising them all along. Then you get to walk this journey together. You'll find there are millions of us waking up to the Gospel, the Good News of grace and identity in Jesus.

Well, enough. Go read. We'll meet you in the Room of Grace.

To Please or to Trust?

*Two roads diverged in a wood, and I, I took the one
less traveled by, and that has made all the difference.*

—Robert Frost

. . . And so the day comes when we are forced to choose. Eventually, we each find ourselves arriving at a pivotal place on our journey with God. We stand before two roads diverging in the woods, and our choice will make all the difference. We may not even realize we are making this choice, but we all make it many times on our journey. It's the most important ongoing decision any of us will make as Christians.

As we're walking down life's road, we arrive at a tall pole with signs pointing in two different directions. The marker leading to the left simply says *Pleasing God*. The one leading to the right reads *Trusting God*. It's hard to choose one over the other, because both roads have a good feel to them. We discover there is no third road and it becomes obvious that we will not be able to jump back and forth between the paths. We must choose one. *Only* one. It will now indelibly mark the way we live.

Pleasing God and *Trusting God* represent the primary and ultimate motives of our hearts, the inner drives or desires that cause us to act in a certain way. These motives, in turn, produce multiple actions:

Motive → Values → Actions

Pleasing God and *Trusting God* are both admirable, but since I can have only one primary motive, I ask myself, "Which of these motives best reflects the relationship I want to have with God?"

In the end, I choose the path marked *Pleasing God*. The *Trusting God* path just seems too, well, passive. I want a fully alive experience with God. The *Pleasing God* path seems like the best way there. I think, *All right then, my mind's made up. I am determined to please God. I so long for Him to be happy with me. I'll discipline myself to achieve this life goal. I know I can do it. Yes, I will do it this time. I will please Him and He will be pleased with me.* So we set off with with renewed confidence. We are immediately comforted to see that the path is well traveled.

In time I come to a door with a sign that reads *Striving to Be All God Wants Me to Be*. These words reflect the values that flow out of the motive of *Pleasing God*, and they describe how we believe we should act. Since my motive is a determination to please God, I will value being all God wants me to be. So, I open the door by turning the knob of Effort. The motive of *Pleasing God* has now produced the value of *Striving to Be All That God Wants Me to Be*. As I enter this enormous room, a hostess with a beautiful smile greets me and says in an almost too polite tone, "Welcome to the Room of Good Intentions."

Oh, yes. I like the ring of this name. I also like being perceived as someone who is well intended. "Well, thanks," I answer. "I think I've found my home. How are you?"

The hostess pauses for a moment and then reaches into her purse to pull out a mask bearing a guarded expression and a thin smile. She puts it on and answers, "Fine. Just fine. And you?"

The entire room gets suddenly quiet, awaiting my answer. "Well, umm, thanks for asking. I'm kind of struggling with some things right now, some areas that don't seem to be in keeping with who I know I'm supposed to be. I'm not really sure I'm doing well on a lot of—" The hostess cuts me off, putting her finger to her lips and handing me a similar mask. I'm not quite sure what to do. I don't really want to put it on, but others in the room are smiling and motioning for me to do so. I want so much to be accepted here that I slowly put it on.

And now everything feels different. I am quickly overcome with the realization that less self-revelation would be a smart game plan here. I realize that no one in this room wants to hear about my struggles, pain, or doubt. If I want to be welcomed here, I better keep my cards closer to my vest and give the appearance of sufficiency. So, I slowly and carefully say the words, "Actually, I'm fine. I'm doing just fine. Thanks." Satisfied, everyone in the room turns back to their conversations.

You see, everyone in the Room of Good Intentions has the value of *Striving to Be All God Wants Them to Be*. They are sincerely determined to be godly. Their value produces actions that are best summarized by an enormous banner on the back wall that reads, *Working on My Sin to Achieve an Intimate Relationship with God*. They have made it their goal to be godly, and they fully expect the same of everyone else in the room.

As I read the words on the banner, I can't help but think, *Sounds a lot like, "Be holy as your heavenly Father is holy."[1] Yep. I'm in the right place. The people here have sincerity, perseverance, courage, diligence, full-hearted fervency, a desire to please God, and a sold-out determination to pursue excellence. Yes, this is the place I've been looking for. Oh, I'm going to make Him so happy. One day soon, we will be close. I just know it!*

Yet, as weeks turn into months, I can't help noticing that many people in this room sound a bit cynical and look pretty tired. Many of them seem alone. And if I catch them when they think no one is looking, I see incredible pain on their faces. Quite a few seem superficial—guarded. After awhile I realize that my thinking has begun shifting too. I no longer feel as comfortable or relaxed here. I have this nagging anxiety that if I don't keep behaving well—if I don't control my sin enough—I'll be on the outs with everyone in the room. And with God!

So, I start investing more effort into sinning less, and I feel better . . . for a while. But the more time I spend in the Room of Good Intentions, the more disappointment I feel. Despite all my striving, all my efforts, I keep sinning! In fact, some days I'm fixated simply on trying *not* to sin. I seem to never be able to get around to doing things to please God. It takes all my energy to avoid doing those things that *displease* Him! Other days I can't seem to do enough. I never get through my list of things to work on. It feels like I am making every effort to please a God who never seems pleased enough! I carry an overwhelming sense of guilt because I have to hide my sin—from everyone in the room and from God. Gradually, almost imperceptibly, the road of *Pleasing God* has turned into *What Must I Do to Keep God Pleased with Me?*

The stifling atmosphere in the room and the tightness of my mask make it hard for me to breathe. I am so tired of pretending and keeping up appearances.

As I search for the door, someone walks up to me and, looking over his shoulder, whispers, "Hey, umm, I'm going to check out that other path back at the crossroads. For the last several years, I've given this room everything I've got, and something's not working for me. You look tired too. You want to go retrace our steps and head out for the Trusting God trail?"

I Took the Road Less Traveled . . .

So back I go to the fork in the road. Hmmm. It still feels wrong to take the road marked *Trusting God*—as if I'd be getting away with something. I look around for a third road, maybe some combination of the two, but no such luck. There are just the two roads. Still. The road of *Trusting God* sure sounds a lot less heroic than the other. A bit ethereal and vague. And it appears to give me nothing much to do other than, well . . . trust. All I ever heard in the Room of Good Intentions was that I have to "sell out, care more, get on fire, buck up, shape up, and tighten up." This road doesn't seem to give me any of that. But I think, *I'm only risking a little time and effort. I can always head back to the Pleasing God path if this turns out to be a dead end. Besides the cracks in my mask are getting bigger and bigger—I don't know how long I can keep bluffing. People have got to be catching on that something's just not right with me. I don't know what else I can do. If this road doesn't take me to where I want to go, I'm cooked. I've got no other game plan. I need answers—real answers—and quickly. I'm running out of time . . . and rubber cement.*

So, I begin walking on life's path with the motive of *Trusting God*. This road is definitely less worn than the other one. I have second thoughts every fifty yards or so. But I cannot bring myself to return to the emptiness of the alternative, so I walk on, looking for that second door. Eventually, I spot it, and as I approach it I read the words on the sign above it:

Living Out of Who God Says I Am. I tilt my head to the side, thinking the phrase might make more sense if I do. *Those are certainly some words, one right after another. What in the world do they mean? It can't mean what I think it means! When do I get to do something here? Where's the part where I get to prove my sincerity? Where are my guidelines? When do I get to give God my best?* I shake my head and stoop down to read what it says on the doorknob . . . Humility.

Suddenly everything snaps into focus. I've tried so hard, I've supplied all the self-effort the other room demanded, yet received nothing but insecurity and duplicity. I've run out of answers, run out of breath, run out of ability, and so I cry out, *God, if anything good is to come out of this whole deal, you will have to do it. I've tried. I can't. I'm so tired. Please God, you will have to give me the life I am dreaming of. I can't keep doing this anymore. I'm losing confidence that this life in you is even possible. Help me. You must make it happen or I am doomed.* With those words I turn the doorknob.

As I step inside, another hostess immediately approaches. She smiles kindly and, with a voice that is at once knowing and reassuring, says softly, "Welcome to the Room of Grace." I answer tentatively, "Thank . . . you."

She presses, "How are *you*?" The room grows quiet.

Well, I've been here before and so, not to be duped twice, I answer, "I'm fine. Pretty fine . . . Who wants to know?" And the room stays quiet. Gun-shy from the first room, I interpret their silence as judgment, and so I yell out, "All right, listen! I'm *not* fine. I haven't been fine for a long time. I'm tired. I feel guilty, lonely, and depressed. I'm sad most of the time and I can't make my life work. And if any of you knew half my daily thoughts, you'd want me out of your little club. So there, I'm doing *not* fine! Thanks for asking!"

I reach for the doorknob to leave, and hear a voice from far back in the crowd. "That's *it*? That's all you've *got*? I'll take your confusion, guilt, and bad thoughts, and I'll raise you compulsive sin and chronic lower back pain! Oh, and I'm in debt up to my ears, and I wouldn't know classical music from a show tune if it jumped up and bit me. You better have more than that puny list if you want to play in my league!"

The greeter smiles and nudges me to say, "I think he means you're welcomed here." Emboldened, I smile, and call back, "Do you struggle with forgetting birthdays?" He walks right up to me all the way from the back, puts his hands on my shoulders and says, "Birthdays? I can't remember my *own*!" Everyone in the room laughs the warm laughter of understanding, and I am ushered into the fold of a sweet family of kind and painfully real people. There is not a mask to be seen anywhere.

As I walk further into the room, I notice a huge banner on the back wall. This one reads: *Standing with God, with My Sin in Front of Me, Working on It Together.* I think, *Wait, this can't be right. How can this be? It sounds presumptuous, care-less. Imagining God with His arm around me as we view my sin together? Come on! Surely they've written it down wrong. I've always been told that my sin is still a barrier between God and me. If it could be true that God actually stands with me, in front of my sin, well, that would change everything. If it were true, God has never moved away from me no matter what I've done! Oh my gosh, I'd have to rethink everything.*[2]

Despite my doubts, I can't help but notice that in this room, the Room of Grace, everyone seems vitally alive. The people are obviously imperfect, full of compromise and struggle, but they're authentic enough to talk about it and ask for help. Many have a level of integrity, maturity, love, laughter, freedom, and vitality that I don't recall seeing in the people in the other room. I feel the start of something I haven't felt in . . . well, as long as I can remember. It's safety or something like it. *Toto, I don't think we're in Kansas anymore.*

Where It All Begins

Okay, let's review. Our motives direct what we value and how we act. For example, if we're motivated by money, we will value lucrative careers and people who can help us make money. That value will then shape how we act. It will influence us to pursue certain education, experience, and jobs. We get the word *motion* from *motive*; our motives ultimately determine our actions. God designed us this way.

Motive → Values → Actions

This timeless sequence is at the very heart of the story of the two roads and the two rooms. Our motive as followers of Christ will either keep us in unresolved sin and immaturity or it will free us into God's astonishing life for us. The key to our maturity and freedom lies in the dominant motive that governs our relationship with God. It all starts with motive.

To Trust Him Is to Please Him

Hebrews 11 declares, "And without faith it is impossible to please God."[3] Did you recognize the two paths in this verse? Did you notice that trusting God pleases God? If our primary motive is *Pleasing God*, we never please Him enough and we never learn trust. That's because life on this road is all about my striving, my effort, my ability to make something happen. But if our primary motive is *Trusting God*, we find out that He is incredibly pleased with us.

So, pleasing God is actually a by-product of trusting God.

But therein lies the problem. We were almost fine with trusting God for the Red Sea deal and the day the sun stood still—but this? Trusting Him with *me!* Yikes, that's asking a lot more than we were bargaining for back in the first room. We'd rather work like a dog to keep Him almost happy than this absurd thought of trying to trust Him with me. *Way too much control given away. Way too much vulnerability. Way too dangerous. Nope, not during my watch.* "Waiter, check please!"

The Deadly Trap

If my life motive is an unwavering determination to *Please God*,

Then my value will be *Striving to Be All God Wants Me to Be*,

And my action will be *Working on My Sin to Achieve an Intimate Relationship with God*.

When we embrace the motive of *Pleasing God* and live in the Room of Good Intentions, we reduce godliness to this formula:

More right behavior + Less wrong behavior = Godliness

This theology comes with a significant problem: It sets us up to fail and to live in hiddenness. It disregards the godliness—righteousness—that God has already placed in us, at infinite cost,[4] and will sabotage our journey. Once

13

we choose the path of *Pleasing God*, the bondage of performance persistently badgers us. Our determination to please God traps us in a formula that affixes our masks so tightly that we'll need jackhammers to get them off!

We can never resolve our sin by working on it. Nor can our striving to sin less keep us from future sins. Oh, we may change behaviors for a while, but as we try to hide the sins we can't control, we are unwittingly inviting blame, shame, denial, fear, and anger to become our constant companions. A theology of more right, less wrong, behavior creates an environment that gives people permission to wear dozens of disguises and masks. It triggers and complicates the chain reaction of unresolved sin, causing us to lose hope. It keeps us immature! Sin-management theology is breaking our hearts. Yet, even though such harmful thinking has let us down a thousand times, we keep trying to control our bad habits and sin. But we cannot hide the reality of what is true about us, because it comes out in our behavior and gets transferred to all we influence.

The apostle Paul tries to help us think our way out of this trap:

> Have some of you noticed that we are not yet perfect? (No great surprise, right?) And are you ready to make the accusation that since people like me, who go through Christ in order to get things right with God, aren't perfectly virtuous, Christ must therefore be an accessory to sin? The accusation is frivolous. If I was "trying to be good," I would be rebuilding the same old barn that I tore down. I would be acting as a charlatan.[5]

Many have spent their entire lives serving God, yet they are broken, defeated, lonely, and full of despair. They have embraced a theology of "rebuilding their old barns"; they have placed all their efforts in "trying to be good."

The first son of Adam and Eve, Cain, chose the path of *Pleasing God* and paid dearly for it. God wanted Cain to acknowledge God's place in his life and to trust God with his intentions. But Cain figured he could make God happy, and that God would make good things happen for him. So Cain worked out a solution on his own terms. He brought offerings that represented his best efforts—the fruit from his fields. Cain was "trying to be good" on his terms. When his offering didn't please God, Cain felt dishonored. He also felt guilt for his sin of disobeying God and offering a self-made sacrifice. Because Cain did not take his sin to God to resolve, it wasn't long before he experienced the inevitable effects of his unresolved sin—he became so filled with shame, blame, and anger that he ended up killing his younger brother, Abel.[6]

Early in his reign, King Saul likely struggled with trusting God, just like the Galatians whom Paul corrected. Saul ended up trying to keep God pleased with him. Saul thought his sacrifice would please God enough to give him success against Israel's enemies. But God said, "To obey is better than sacrifice." He knew Saul's obedience would be the evidence of his trust.[7]

Pleasing God is an incredibly good longing. It always will be. But it can't be our primary motivation, or it will imprison our hearts. *Pleasing is not a means to our personal godliness, it is the fruit of our godliness for it is the fruit of trust. We will never please God through our efforts to become godly. Rather, we will only please God—and become godly—when we trust God.* If we strive to please God by solving our sin, we are back at the same insufficient square one that put us in need of

15

a savior. And we are stuck with our talents, skill, desire, ability, longing, chutzpah, diligence, and resolve to make it happen. Now we've got habañera sauce on our cornflakes.

What value, then, flows from the motive of *Trusting God*? When our motive is *Trusting God*, our value will be *Living Out of Who God Says I Am*. Have we already been changed? Yes. As day is from night, we have changed. We have received a new heart, for crying out loud! We have a brand-new core identity. We have already been changed, and now we get to mature into who we already are.[8]

An Identity Too Valuable to Forfeit

God paid an infinite price to buy us back, to redeem us, and to give us a new identity.[9] So, He gets deeply disappointed when we choose not to believe what He says is now true about us. He values our high-priced identity, and He wants us to do the same. How can we show that we value our identity? Please read these words slowly: *By trusting what He says is true about us.*

If my motive is *Trusting God*, then my value will be *Living Out of Who God Says I Am*, and my action will be *Standing with God, with My Sin in Front of Us, Working on It Together*.

Nature provides many examples of this incredible discrepancy between who we appear to be and who we truly are. Consider the caterpillar. If we brought a caterpillar to a biologist and asked him to analyze it and describe its DNA, he would tell us, "I know this looks like a caterpillar to you, but scientifically, according to every test, including DNA, this is fully and completely a butterfly." Wow! God has wired into a creature that looks nothing like a butterfly, a perfectly complete butterfly "identity." And because the caterpillar is a butterfly in essence, it will one day display the behavior and attributes of a butterfly. The caterpillar matures into what is already true about it. In the meantime, berating the caterpillar for not being more like a butterfly is not only futile, it will probably hurt his tiny ears!

So it is with us. God has given us the DNA of godliness. We are saints. Righteous. Nothing we do will make us more righteous than we already are. Nothing we do will alter this reality. God knows our DNA. He knows that we are "Christ in me." And now He is asking us to join Him in what He knows is true!

Paul asked the Galatian community if they could remember who made this new identity:

> Can't you see the central issue in all this? It is not what you and I do—submit to circumcision, reject circumcision. It is what God is doing, and *He* is creating something totally new, a free life![10] (emphasis added)

Many of us would answer Paul's question by saying, "No, I can't see the central issue in all this." We actually think that we achieve godliness through striving. We actually think that what we do can "create something totally new." We think we're a match for sin . . . that all we need to do is work a little harder . . . do a little more. We value striving, because we trust our own assessment of who we are instead of God's.[11]

The Great Disconnect

Of course, many people talk as if they have taken the *Trusting God* road, but in reality they live in the Room of Good Intentions. Why do so many people say the right thing, but then live the wrong life? We call this sweeping reality in the church today The Great Disconnect.

The three stories that follow come from among hundreds that we have been told. We've intentionally selected stories from people employed in Christian work, because if we can see the disconnect between talking and living at this level, we may conclude that this chasm exists everywhere in the body of Christ.

Story one. At a training forum a woman walked up to us in tears and said, "I am very frightened and I don't know what to do, but I have to tell somebody. I am so embarrassed. We are missionaries, with three children, and for over two years, my husband, who is a teacher and executive in our mission, has engaged in major deceit and fraud. He said he wouldn't tell you, but I have to. I cannot live like this any longer."

Question: How can people who move their family to a foreign country to serve God and who rise to leadership positions in their missions and teach truth in scores of situations live in such duplicity? How can what this man believes and teaches others have so little to do with what he actually believes about himself?

Story two. Matthew is a professional counselor. He feels unloved, underappreciated, and lonely. He has been fighting depression for more than five years. He is getting very tired and is losing the strength to keep performing as if everything is okay. But his mask has not worn out to the point where lying is beneath him. Recently he told his organization that he was going on vacation, but the truth was that he was checking himself into a rehab clinic in order to get treatment.

Question: How can a competent Christian counselor deceive others about his severe need for professional care, while attempting to offer others similar care?

Story three. Doug and Wanda presented a very impressive image of their relationship. They were marriage and family retreat speakers, and he taught future pastors marriage and family courses in a seminary. Yet Doug told us, "I am deeply angry with my wife. I have been for a long time. But my anger is no match for her longstanding disappointment in who I am and have become. She withdraws from me. Our physical relationship is almost nonexistent. We continually speak to scores of couples and families, but we are bluffing about our own marriage."

Question: How can a man and woman with such key responsibilities for transferring truth to others know next to nothing about applying that truth to their own marriage and family? What is likely to happen to those who are being influenced by these kinds of leaders?

Jesus warned us about this very thing when he said: "Be wary of false preachers who smile a lot, dripping with practiced sincerity. . . . Don't be impressed with charisma; look for character. Who preachers *are* is the main thing, not what they say."[12] Erwin McManus catches this fundamental issue when he says, "What I said on Sunday wasn't nearly as important as what I did."[13]

A missionary executive couple, a seasoned counselor, professional teachers and retreat speakers. Each projected a marriage, a life, and a ministry that was "together," healthy. Each can quote Scripture on demand, teach excellent Bible lessons, and instruct others about what it means to be "in Christ." Together they influence thousands who look to them for spiritual direction. Yet, their masked reality tells a very different story about what they really believe about themselves and their circumstances.

Taking the road marked *Pleasing God*, many, many Christians never understand or live out what it means to be "in Christ Jesus." The *Pleasing God* path creates the fearful and hidden environment that produces this disconnect.

These stories demonstrate that our well-crafted, religiously correct words are the least reliable clues about our motives. If we want to determine our real motives, we need to look at our values and actions. In other words, if I:

- Value together-looking, sanitized appearances,

- Value neatly packaged people and can't stand imperfection,

- Act to control my children in public so they'll make me look put together, or

- Camouflage or hide my own unresolved sin from others,

then, I'm motivated by trying to please God . . . and I need everyone else to know that I please God. I feel driven to maintain the appearance of living this God life. It's a motivation everything else must serve.

The New Testament "Gamble"

We discover in the Room of Grace that the almost unthinkable has happened. God has shown all of His cards. He reveals a breathtaking protection that brings us out of hiding. In essence, God says, "What if I tell them who they are? What if I take away any element of fear in condemnation, judgment, or rejection? What if I tell them I love them, will always love them? That I love them right now, no matter what they've done, as much as I love my only Son? That there's nothing they can do to make my love go away?

"What if I tell them there are no lists? What if I tell them I don't keep a log of past offenses, of how little they pray, how often they've let me down, made promises that they don't keep? What if I tell them they are righteous, with my righteousness, right now? What if I tell them they can stop beating themselves up? That they can stop being so formal, stiff, and jumpy around me? What if I tell them I'm *crazy* about them? What if I tell them, even if they run to the ends of the earth and do the most horrible, unthinkable things, that when they come back, I'd receive them with tears and a party?

"What if I tell them that if I am their Savior, they're going to heaven no matter what—it's a done deal? What if I tell them they have a new nature—saints, not saved sinners who should now 'buck-up and be better if they were any kind of Christians, after all He's done for you!' What if I tell them that I actually live in them now? That I've put my love, power, and nature inside of them, at their disposal? What if I tell them that they don't have to put on a mask? That it is ok to be who they are at this moment, with all their junk. That they don't need to to pretend about how close we are, how much they pray or don't, how much Bible they read or don't. What if they knew they don't have to look over their shoulder for fear if things get too good, the other shoe's gonna drop?

"What if they knew I will never, ever use the word *punish* in relation to them? What if they knew that when they mess up, I will never 'get back at them?' What if they were convinced that bad circumstances aren't my way of evening the score for taking advantage of me? What if they knew the basis of our friendship isn't how little they sin, but how much they let me love them? What if I tell them they can hurt my heart, but that I never hurt theirs? What if I tell them I like Eric Clapton's music too? What if I tell them I never really liked the Christmas handbell deal with the white gloves? What if I tell them they can open their eyes when they pray and still go to heaven? What if I tell them there is no secret agenda, no trapdoor? What if I tell them it isn't about their self-effort, but about allowing me to live my life through them?"

When you stand at the crossroads, you decide which road to choose largely upon how you see God's "gamble." *Do I really believe this stuff will hold up—for me?* This is the way of life in the Room of Grace. It is the way home to healing, joy, peace, fulfillment, contentment, and release into God's dreams for us. It almost feels like we're stealing silverware from the king's house, doesn't it? Truth is, the king paid a lot so that you wouldn't have to try to steal any silverware. He gets to *give* it to you; and other stuff so big and good and beautiful that we couldn't even begin to stuff it into our bag of loot. Wow! It takes the eyes some adjustment to look into such light, huh?

Changing or Maturing?

If we refuse to enter the Room of Grace, we will constantly be striving in the Room of Good Intentions. We will strive to change into something we are not yet: godly. In the Room of Grace we grow up and mature into something that is already true about us: godly. The first room creates a works-based, performance-driven relationship with God and puts the responsibility on our resources. The second room places the responsibility on the resources of God.

God is not interested in changing you. He already has. The new DNA is set. God wants you to believe that He has already changed you so that He can get on with the process of maturing you into who you already are. Trust opens the way for this process—for God to bring you to maturity. If you do not trust God, you can't mature, because your focus is messed up. You're still trying to change enough to be labeled godly.

Does the God who lavishly provides you with His own presence, his Holy Spirit, working things in your lives you could never do for yourselves, does He do these things because of your strenuous moral striving or because you trust Him to do them in you?[14]

If you are living in the Room of Grace, you aren't making desperate attempts to improve yourself. You know you cannot change yourself; you can only mature because of who you already are: a spiritually new creation born of the Spirit, a saint maturing into the image of Christ.

Those inside the Room of Grace place their effort just where God can use it. Ponder the contrast of how Effort works in the two rooms. On the road of *Pleasing God*, Effort gets me into the Room of Good Intentions. On the road of *Trusting God*, Effort is found inside the Room of Grace. Effort is never a means of pleasing God or getting God's grace or changing myself. Effort is a response that God uses to work together with me on my sin, to mature into that person with whom He is already pleased. Effort born out of striving to please God never ceases to tire us. Effort born out of resting in His pleasure never ceases to renew us.

Pleasing God with the Right Motive

Pleasing God is a wonderful desire, but it never gives entry to the Room of Grace. Now, inside the Room of Grace, we finally can honor our yearning to please God.

When we reverse trusting and pleasing, it's like switching "trust and obey" to "obey and trust." Placing obedience before trust locks us into a mindset of obeying to please God, to earn His favor, His pleasure.

If we do not start with trusting who God says we are, we will end up trusting in our own resources to try to please God. This kind of self-sufficient mindset nauseates God.[15]

The following statements do not gain us entry into the Room of Grace; they describe the privilege and fulfillment of living in it.

- "Live a life worthy of the Lord [that you] may please Him in every way."[16]

- "Offer your bodies as living sacrifices, holy and pleasing to God."[17]

- "The gifts you sent . . . are an acceptable sacrifice, pleasing to God."[18]

- "Live in order to please God, as in fact you are living."[19]

Now, we have pleasing in its proper place. The citizens in the Room of Grace get the privilege of experiencing the pleasure of God, because they have pleased God by trusting Him.

The Goal of Life

John still remembers sitting down with Bill more than eighteen years ago when Bill was his boss. John was a young, gifted preacher, complete with four years of seminary, a snappy briefcase, and a bookshelf full of impressive-looking, scholarly books. He told Bill, "I think there are about two or three issues that I haven't yet overcome. They're not too complex or difficult. Once they get solved I really think I can be used by God in a big way."

John expected Bill to respond, "Well, let's get to work on those. What are they? Let's look at them one at a time and solve them so you can really take off." Instead Bill looked at John for a long time and then slowly said the words to John that God has used to change the entire focus of how he lives the Christian life. "John, then I hope that you never, ever completely solve those issues. You will become self-dependent. You will become self-sufficient. The goal is not for you to get all of your 'stuff' solved. You never will. There is an endless list of stuff. God is gracious to reveal only a snippet at a time. The goal is to learn to depend on—to trust—what God says is true about you, so that together you can begin dealing with that stuff."

John was headed straight for the Room of Good Intentions where The Great Disconnect spreads like a viral bug. Worse, the *Pleasing God* path John intended to travel would have produced two or three hundred more unresolved sin issues. But John learned about a road less traveled by. And that has made all the difference.

If you have been searching for the hope described in this chapter, come with us further into the Room of Grace. Discover how God's power to handle sin in this environment of grace not only resolves sin, but also allows God to do in us far beyond what we could even ask or imagine.[20]

Did You Discover?

- *Pleasing God* and *Trusting God* represent the ultimate motives of our hearts.

- If my life motive is an unwavering determination to *Please God*

  o Then my value will be striving to be all God wants me to be

  o And my action will be working on my sin to achieve an intimate relationship with God.

- When we strive to sin less, we don't sin less.

- *Pleasing God* is an incredibly good longing. It always will be. It just can't be our primary motivation, or it will imprison our hearts.

- If my motive is *Trusting God*

  o Then my value will be living out of who God says I am

  o And my action will be standing with God, with my sin in front of us, working on it together.

- Many people say they have taken the path of *Trusting God* but have ended up in the Room of Good Intentions. This is called The Great Disconnect.

- Our response to the New Testament "Gamble" becomes a limitless test—telling us which road we've chosen.

- God is not interested in changing the Christian. He already has.

- Trust opens the way for God to bring us to maturity. If we do not trust, we do not mature.

- If we do not start with trusting who God says we are, we will end up with trusting in our own resources to try to please God.

One Session Study Guide
Experiencing Two Roads, Two Rooms

Before you begin:

1. Take time to soak up all the stories and thoughts in this booklet. This will be the basis for answering the following questions. You may want to review the "Did You Discover?" questions at the end of the chapter as well. To dig even further into the background for this chapter, look up the related Scripture passages in the endnotes.

2. Get together with your group. If you are a part of a large group (such as a church school class), you may have a teacher or leader facilitate the experience. If you're doing this in a small group setting, anyone can lead the group by following the directions in this section.

3. Consider the following guidelines for making the most of your group experience:

   • When you are directed to form a small group for an activity, select people you know at least a little. If you are placed in a pair or trio with people you don't know, take a couple minutes to introduce yourselves. This will give you a good starting place for this activity.

- Follow the directions carefully, particularly as they relate to discussion in your small group of two or three. These directions have been designed to provide safe boundaries so you can share appropriately with others.

- The truths you discover during this experience apply to many other areas of life. Practice what you learn outside of this session together.

- Above all, don't be anxious about the group activity in this guide. It is not one of those scary, "stand up in front of the group and share your life" experiences. That's not to say what you learn will be fluffy, surface-level stuff. The experiences can be life-changing.

For the Group Leader

If you are the designated leader, please follow these guidelines to ensure a positive experience for all participants.

1. Make sure each person has a copy of this booklet before the session.

2. You are a facilitator for this, not a teacher. Follow the instructions closely and fight any temptation to expand on the material provided. This is a place for experiential learning, *not* lecture.

3. Don't worry if some are unable to answer two questions. Unanswered questions are part of the discovery process.

4. When dividing into groups of two or three, it can be helpful if participants know each other, but it is not essential. Groups of three will allow you to complete the

session in an hour. If you have additional time, groups of up to five people will also work well.

5. Close the session with prayer.

Introducing the Experience

In this session, we're going to apply TrueFaced principles in an activity we call "Connecting." This experience connects two things that most of us have a hard time joining: What I *say* is true about me with how I actually *live*. We call this kind of fragmented living—saying one thing is true but living as if another thing is true—The Great Disconnect. This activity will help you experience The Great Connect as you enter the Room of Grace.

For an Enjoyable Experience

In order to make this experience excellent and beneficial to all, consider the following guidelines for your small and large group time:

- Allow other group members to answer their questions. Do not interrupt.

- Allow other group members to "keep" their answers. Do not correct. This is a *discovery* process, not a declaration of fact. No one should have to defend any answer.

- Allow the other group members to experience safety. Do not discuss their answers outside your group, unless they give you permission to do so.

Processing the "Connecting" Experience in small group

- Begin by forming a small group with one or two partners. Groups of three work best. This experience should take approximately 30 minutes.

- On your own, think about and write answers to two of the "Connecting Questions" in the section. You need not write out the whole answer, because it's about your story, so a few words will likely remind you of the entire answer.

- After everyone's finished writing, take turns sharing your answers with your small group. Allow about five minutes per group member for this sharing time.

- When everyone has shared, pray for one another to practice "connecting" each time you encounter an opportunity to live out of who God says you are.

Connecting Questions

1. What thoughts or circumstances most often cause you to stay trapped in the Room of Good Intentions? What frees you into the Room of Grace?

2. What are the circumstances that cause you to wear masks? How would "believing who God says you are" gradually help you to remove your masks?

3. Have you ever tried to get out of the Room of Good Intentions, only to have others try to stop you? What was that like? How did that make you feel? (Please don't mention names.)

4. What might it cost you to connect what God says is true about you with how you actually live? How do you do that?

Processing the "Connecting" Experience in large group

Get back together as a large group and spend a little time answering the following question. Allow time for everyone who desires to share to do so.

1. What did you just experience in your smaller groups?

2. What questions did your small group interaction raise for you that you need to process further?

3. What will it take for you to take next steps in this process of discovering the Room of Grace?

Note: For more on stepping into this new grace-life, check out the book *TrueFaced* and the accompanying experience guide, and the *TrueFaced Message* CD, all available at www. TrueFaced.com.

Endnotes

1. Matthew 5:48. See also Leviticus 19:2; Deuteronomy 18:13; 1 Peter 1:14-16.

2. Romans 5:8; Matthew 28:20b; Hebrews 13:5; Acts 18:9-10.

3. Hebrews 1l:6. The word "faith" is the noun form of the word "believe" or "trust." Note the connection here.

4. Philippians 3:9. Not only does it disregard the righteousness we already have in Christ, but it explicitly contradicts the principle Paul enunciates in Galatians 3:1-3 and Colossians 2:6; that is, that we received Christ by faith and that is also how we are to live in him!

5. Galatians 2:16-18, msg.

6. Genesis 4:4-5. The problem was not just the offering, but something was wrong within the motive of Cain himself.

7. 1 Samuel 13:5-15; Hebrews 3:18-19; 4:2. The link between trust and obedience is unmistakable.

8. I am blessed, Ephesians 1:3; I am chosen and holy, 1:4; I am adopted, 1:5; I am forgiven, 1:7; I am favored, 1:7-8; I am close to God, 2:13; I am loved, 3:17-19; I am promised great things, 3:6; I am cherished, 5:29.

9. Ephesians 1:3-14.

10. Galatians 6:15, msg.

11. Proverbs 3:5-6.

12. Matthew 7:15-16, msg.

13. Erwin McManus, *An Unstoppable Force* (Loveland, Colo.: Group Publishing, 2001), p. 156.

14. Galatians 3:5, msg.

15. Revelation 3:15-22. The word in verse 16 literally is "vomit" rather than "spit," as it is often more politely translated. Politeness, however, masks God's revulsion with such lukewarm self-sufficience!

16. Colossians 1:10-12, nasb.

17. Romans 12:1-2. Paul specifically references the truth taught earlier in this chapter in that the word he uses for "transformed" is a form of the Greek verb from which we get "metamorphosis," which is nothing other than the process of maturing into what you were designed to be!

18. Philippians 4:18.

19. 1 Thessalonians 4:1.

20. Ephesians 3:20-21.

About Leadership Catalyst / TrueFaced

One word has the power to catalyze greatness in an individual, an organization, or a nation: Trust. Surveys show that trust is the #1 requirement for influence in life and leadership. But for many, trust has been hard to come by or misplaced. There is a painful Trust Gap . . . and it appears to be widening in many arenas of the church, business, education, missions, government, and even family life.

The mission of Leadership Catalyst / TrueFaced is *to build and restore trust in leaders and those who follow them.* Established in 1995, Leadership Catalyst / TrueFaced is recognized as an international resource for helping leaders of all ages develop TrueFaced communities of grace, where character, authenticity, and influence can flourish.

For the individual, Leadership Catalyst / TrueFaced offers a variety of resource tools to help you build trust in your friendships, your family, and your community.

For the organization, Leadership Catalyst / TrueFaced has designed a groundbreaking process to help leaders and teams bridge the Trust Gap. The *TrueFaced Process* is a foundational, baseline process, functioning much like a computer operating system that accelerates the programs in a computer. Therefore, The *TrueFaced Process* is designed to enrich and leverage the other programs that are already embraced within the organization. Delivery of The *TrueFaced Process* is implemented through your organization's leaders, who are trained in TrueFaced leadership intensives.

For more information and resources,
see www.TrueFaced.com

Email: info@TrueFaced.com

Voice 888-249-0700 Toll-free in North America

About the Authors

BILL THRALL is the Vice Chair, co-author and leadership mentor for Leadership Catalyst/TrueFaced since 1995, having formerly served as a CPA and an influential pastor. Bill's genuine desire to see relational health in those he works with has been vital in setting the tone of the organization. His wisdom has been penned throughout the entire series of *The Ascent of a Leader*, *Beyond Your Best*, and *TrueFaced* books.

BRUCE MCNICOL portrays truth through stories, metaphors, and wisdom statements, which fill the best-selling resources he and his friends have co-authored. As president and co-founder for Leadership Catalyst/TrueFaced, Bruce is passionate to see tens of thousands of environments of grace thriving around the world—in families, businesses, organizations, sports, churches, armed forces and governments.

JOHN LYNCH is a great communicator, a talented writer and a vital member of the Leadership Catalyst/TrueFaced staff. In addition to speaking internationally with Bill and Bruce, John has co-authored a number of books with them, including *TrueFaced*. He presents Leadership Catalyst's powerful *TrueFaced Message* on both CD & DVD. John also serves as a teaching pastor at Open Door Fellowship in Phoenix, Arizona.

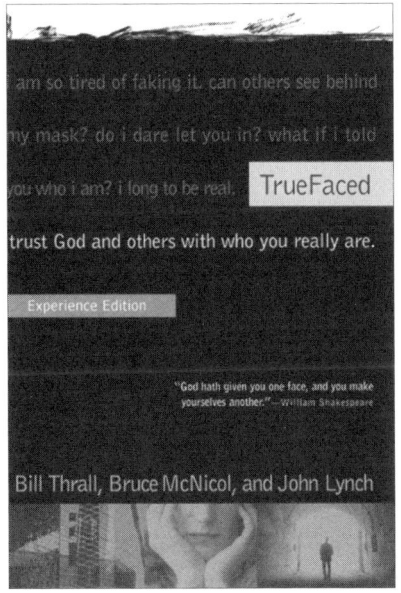

For individual or small group use:

TrueFaced Experience Guide
for use with the TrueFaced Experience DVD and Experience Edition book

In eight, interactive sessions, you'll find real stories and tools to help you discover what it means to live in grace and to be real with yourself, God, and others..

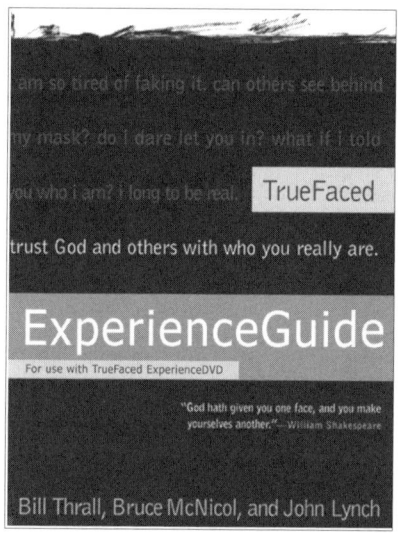

Move into the room of Grace

For individual or small group use:

The Ascent of a Leader
How Ordinary Relationships Develop Extraordinary Character and Influence

In this practical book you'll discover what it takes to become a great leader: character and capacity.

A leader people want to follow

"In a world filled with so much cynicism and fear, this is one book that definitely will fill your heart and soul with hope and joy."
- Jim Kouzes
co-author
The Leadership Challenge

call 888-249-0700 or visit TrueFaced.com for more information

For individual or small group use:

Beyond Your Best
Develop Your Relationships,
Fulfill Your Destiny

If you've ever felt like there must be more to life—like you were meant to do something more significant—you're right.

The process of character